SPEAKING ALOUD -RAINBOW BRIDGE COLLECTIO

©JULIE M GRABHAM

Speaking Aloud – Rainbow Bridge Collection

This collection of original poems is dedicated to Dobby, Odin, Lola and all the precious paws that have left to walk over Rainbow Bridge.

" Our favourite hellos and hardest goodbyes".

A percentage of the sale of this books goes to CHILL, Cancer Helps In Local Lives

Speaking Aloud – Rainbow Bridge Collection

1. Waiting for you
2. Meet at the bridge
3. The saviour of you
4. One of a kind
5. Pawprints on my heart
6. Rainbow Bridge came calling
7. Stay in my heart
8. Greet me at the bridge
9. Turn the clock back
10. Heaven's gate
11. Goodbye for now
12. When your heart stopped still
13. Don't cry
14. Just a dog
15. Signs
16. Visiting hours
17. Grief knocks
18. Lola
19. Dobby
20. Odin

Waiting for you

Your bowl just sits there waiting

For you to come right back.

Your treats are scattered ready

For you to sniff and track.

Your bed is full and fluffy

Your toys are nearby,

Your blanket is on the sofa

Where you always lie.

The garden door is open

For you to wander out,

The floor is clean and ready

For your muddy paws no doubt.

We're all just waiting and praying

That rainbow bridge has turned you away

And we'll get to hold you close again

For at least another day.

Meet at the bridge

Rainbow bridge brings me sadness

Yet I bet it's a beautiful place

Full of pets just so happy.

With smiles upon their face.

It's where our pets pass over

When life on earth is done

No cruelty or heartache

Only love and lots of fun.

Our animals are not afraid to go there

Over the bridge they gladly step

Knowing that their days will be full

Of playing with other pets.

It's us who fear the journey

Became we know it's far away

But out pets will be always with us

Until we meet at the bridge some day.

The saviour of you

Unless you've loved a pet

You may never know the feeling

Of how when they go to rainbow bridge

Your whole world is left reeling.

Absolutely nothing, can try and soften the blow

Or prepare you for the fatal day.

Those words of comfort won't help

That kind-hearted people will say.

Your head will have that nagging feel

A throbbing you just can't shake

Your body will long for sleep

But you'll lie all night awake.

The grief will hit you in waves

As you are overwhelmingly sad

No other pet will replace

The love that you once had.

A new pet isn't instead of

It's because of the special one

Yes there'll be more heartache

But it's a risk that you should run.

As your heart is full of goodness

Another pet deserves to be loved by you

Your new love will help to heal your heart

And be the saviour of you.

One of a kind

Today I've cried like no other
I can't bear life without you
Your constantly on my mind
In everything I do.

I'll sell my soul to the devil
There's not a promise I won't make
I'll do whatever is available
No challenge I won't take.

My need for you is desperate
My love just runs so deep.
I'd give my all to have you back
A wish that's just too steep.

I'll never ever forget you
You'll be forever in my mind
Our bond can never be broken
It's simply one of a kind.

Pawprints on my heart

Hold my heart so gently

Carefully look up close

You'll see small kisses everywhere

Of the loved ones that I've lost.

Amongst all those kisses

Are paw prints on my heart

Just a special reminder

That we'll never be apart

Rainbow Bridge came calling

Rainbow bridge came calling
I wasn't ready for goodbye,
I held your paw for the last time
Tears flowing from my eyes.

I said how much I love you,
But you already knew that so,
My heart was already in pieces
As I prepared to let you go.

You passed away so quickly
It was your time to leave.
You gave a look that told me
Oh Mam, please don't grieve.

For your time on earth was wonderful
Your life was full of love.
You'll always walk besides us
Look out for signs from above.

Stay in my heart

I see your paw prints on the sand

On the beach you loved to play

I feel your presence near me

Every single day.

I swear I see your tail wag

As I open the front door

Then it suddenly hits me

You're not here anymore.

I sometimes hear you barking

Just a short distance away

I look but I can't find you

Your name I softly say.

I close my eyes to see you

I long to feel your touch

I never knew that loving you

Could hurt my heart so much.

One day we'll be together

And then we'll never part.

Until that special moment

Please stay in my heart

Greet me at the bridge

The bridge that's full of colours

Where all our animals go

Is such a fun and vibrant place

There's no sadness there or woe.

No animal feels pain there

No suffering they will see.

It's full of peace and endless love

Where they all run around free.

The only thing that's missing

Is us humans who love them so

We will be reunited

When it's our time to go.

We know that when that day comes

They'll wait at the bridge with glee

Tails will soon be wagging

As they greet you and me.

Turn the clock back

If only I could turn the clock back

I do things differently

I wouldn't waste a moment

Of the time you spent with me.

I wouldn't moan about the weather

When we had to go for a walk

I wouldn't wish for time to fly

As our coats got soaked.

I wouldn't huff and roll over

When you try to wake me up

I wouldn't pull a face

When you slobber in my cup.

Instead, I'd treasure each second

Wishing you would live forever

Praying that my hardest goodbye

Won't be said now or never.

Heaven's Gate

Today I've had a day pass
To a very special place
A chance to see you once again
And kiss your precious face.

I'll hold you oh so tightly
Afraid to let you go
Telling you how much
Everyone has missed you so.

I'll give you all the updates
Of what we've been up to
Always making sure
That you know we still love you.

The time will pass so quickly
As I stand at heaven's gate
Dreading saying goodbye again
And ending this precious date

But I know deep down, I don't need a day
To come and visit you
You're by my side all the time
In everything I do.

Goodbye for now

I would never ever be ready

To say goodbye for now,

As I kissed your cheek a final time

My eternal love I vowed.

I know you're no longer suffering

I know you're no longer in pain,

My complete heartbreak

Is undoubtedly heaven's gain.

I'll always pause and wonder

If there was something else I could do,

Anything to make it clear

That I will forever love you.

When I'm in my darkest days

And my tears fall like rain,

I know you'll hold our love safe

Until we meet again.

When your heart stopped still

When your heart stopped still

My world changed in a beat.

Yet life carries on

For all the people that I meet.

Sometimes I can't go on

Without you by my side,

I need your strength

For every journey that I ride.

I close my eyes

Memories I see

I soak up your love

I know you're next to me.

I cling to every sign

You send along my way,

Knowing that we'll meet again,

How I long for that day.

I'll live my life

The best that I can do.

Every moment nearer

Until I'm back with you.

Don't cry

Don't sit and cry for me

I haven't gone away.

I'm up here, watching over you

I'm by your side each day.

Don't weep for me in sadness

Think of what we had

Smile at all the memories

How our love made us so glad.

Don't wallow over what could have been

If I was still alive with you.

Just know that I am sending strength

For everything you do.

Please smile as you remember

To be happy isn't wrong.

No distance will divide us

Our love is just so strong.

Just a dog

You're more than just a dog to me
You're my special mate.
I tell you all my troubles
Your listening skills are great.

You give me unconditional love
I return that back to you.
You're always right by my side
In everything I do.

You make me smile when I am sad
You get me out of bed.
You always know the magic time
When you expect to be fed.

You're more than just a dog to me
I knew it from the start.
I'll love you now and ever more
Your paw prints are in my heart.

Signs

Signs are what we look for

When we've lost someone dear.

Signs are what we cling to

Just to know that they are near,

A sign could be a rainbow

Bright and beautiful in the sky

Or suddenly seeing a robin

That appears close by.

A sign will give you comfort

Perhaps it's a butterfly,

For me the greatest sign of all

Is a white feather nearby.

The signs appear from nowhere

They come out of the blue.

Signs are a gift from a loved one

Make sure you say thank you.

Heaven's visiting hours

If only heaven had visiting hours

I'd pop up there for a day

Just to see my loved ones

I promise I won't stay.

A kiss and a full embrace

To soak up the smell of their hair

To hold their face in my hands

To tell them how much I care.

Please open the gates for a while

To the stairs of up above.

Give me a chance to hold onto

All the ones I love.

Grief knocks

Just as I was finding quiet time

A quiet knock came at the door

I closed my eyes and ignored it

Then it knocked some more.

I still didn't get up to answer

Hoping it would go away

Let me in, I know you're in there

I could hear a soft voice say.

Oh please not today I begged

I just needed to have a break,

But the knocking became relentless

No for answer it wouldn't take.

Reluctantly I gave in

And welcomed my guest inside

The emotions suddenly engulfed me

Overflowing with no guide.

Then the comfort started

A feeling of relief

As I bade farewell to my visitor

The one we all call grief.

Lola

Oh, Lola we were not ready

For you to make your way

Going over Rainbow Bridge

We wanted many more days.

Every moment with you was precious

You were such a funny girl.

A million miles an hour

Greeting everyone in a whirl.

You came on so many adventures

Up mountains and even on a canal boat.

You made us laugh with how different you looked

Every time we trimmed your coat.

You were such a clever girl too

Learning tricks so easily

We loved you oh so dearly

You were one of our family.

How will we cope without you

Life just feels so sad

One day we'll smile about you

As we remember the love we had.

Dobby

Dobby you were our first dog

We learnt so much from you

You showed us how to love a dog

And all the naughty things you do.

You loved to chew the remote control

And you'd sit on your waiting chair,

Smothering us in kisses

If we dared to sit right there.

We'd often ask where's Dobby gone

When under the blankets you hid

Your wagging tail would thump like mad

With everything you did.

You absolutely broke our hearts

When over the bridge you went

But we always smile as we appreciate

Rosie, Odin and Indo were Dobby sent.

Odin

Odin you were such a superstar

You brought us so much joy.

You knocked us out with your kisses

Our very precious boy.

When I supported your birth in rescue

We didn't know what that would mean.

When you were the only brown boy

In the litter called Famous fourteen.

You always knew when it was food time

Is your belly hungry we'd say

You simply adored our Rosie

Playing with your soulmate every day.

Our hearts were truly shattered

When you went to Rainbow Bridge that day

But Odin you'll always be our special boy

And in our hearts you'll always stay,

Thank you to my family and friends for supporting me every step of every journey. I have the best cheerleaders!

Printed in Great Britain
by Amazon

58824450R00020